To my favorite aunt and the best travel agent on the planet!
I ♥ you,
Patricia

xoxo

You are Never Broken Beyond Repair: Reclaiming Your Life and Your Light flows out of a full and transcendent recovery. The author strings together images, wise advice and prompts which encourage the reader to claim and create her own story.

Enough space is allowed for the readers to bring in their experiences to explore identity, self-silencing, shadow, suppression of anger, and the path to embodiment.

O'Connor's well-crafted prompts and questions are tools which, with practice, help the reader cultivate courage and approach the present with an open heart.

This is a book meant to be saved, with notes taken and read over and over again. Absolutely beautiful.

Kimberli McCallum, M.D.
Fellow, American Psychiatric Association
Certified Eating Disorders Specialist
Founder, McCallum Place Treatment Centers

NEVER BROKEN BEYOND REPAIR

Reclaiming Your Life and Your Light

NEVER BROKEN BEYOND REPAIR
RECLAIMING YOUR LIFE AND YOUR LIGHT

By Julie O'Connor
SET SAIL PUBLISHING

Published by Set Sail Publishing, St. Louis, MO

Copyright ©2016 Julie O'Connor

ALL RIGHTS RESERVED.

No part of this publication may be reproduced, stored in a retrieval system, or transmitted in any form or by any means, electronic, mechanical, photocopying, recording, scanning, or otherwise, except as permitted under Section 107 or 108 of the 1976 United States Copyright Act, without the prior written permission of the Publisher. Requests to the Publisher for permission should be addressed to info@JulieOJourneys.com

LIMIT OF LIABILITY/DISCLAIMER OF WARRANTY:

While the publisher and author have used their best efforts in preparing this book, they make no representations or warranties with respect to the accuracy or completeness of the contents of this book and specifically disclaim any implied warranties of merchantability or fitness for a particular purpose. No warranty may be created or extended by sales representatives or written sales materials. The advice and strategies contained herein may not be suitable for your situation. You should consult with a professional where appropriate. Neither the publisher nor author shall be liable for any loss of profit or any other commercial damages, including but not limited to special, incidental, consequential, or other damages.

Cover and Interior design: Davis Creative, DavisCreative.com

Library of Congress Control Number: 2015914895
ISBN: 978-0-9968078-1-4

ATTENTION CORPORATIONS, UNIVERSITIES, COLLEGES AND PROFESSIONAL ORGANIZATIONS: Quantity discounts are available on bulk purchases of this book for educational, gift purposes, or as premiums for increasing magazine subscriptions or renewals. Special books or book excerpts can also be created to fit specific needs. For information, please contact info@JulieOJourneys.com

Give thanks . . .

DEDICATION

For Renée Allen, a calm in the eye of a tumultuous teenage storm — It took a few years to get here, but I am now doing the work that I set out to do. Thank you for pushing me past the illusionary sparkle and shine.

For my nearest and dearest friend, Bonnie — Words are simply inadequate. Your endless encouragement has served as a life vest in some high and choppy waters. I will forever treasure the rare gift that is our friendship.

For my sisters Mary, Kathleen and Susan — Fate made us family, but loyalty and unconditional love made us friends. I'd share a bathroom with you girls all over again!

For my brothers — I am fairly certain that you three could never quite make "heads or tails" of me. You each, in your own way, have taught me something about what it means to be a woman in this world. Homer, Sarge and Buster Purple, Dad would be proud.

For both of my parents, who are now resting in some long-overdue and hard-earned peace — I know that I was beyond confusing and confounding. I know that, on most days, I was just too much for you to handle. I know that I was, in your words, "different than the other six," and I now know that it is OK to be different. Mom and Dad, I love you both. Without you, I quite simply would not be me.

For Kim B. — Thank you for teaching me to taste my words and to tame the torch. It is, without a doubt, all good.

continued . . .

For the ever-evolving cast of characters who I have been blessed to call my girlfriends — I have laughed with and learned from each and every one of you. Even when a relationship lasts but a season, I am grateful and certain that our paths converge for a reason beyond my immediate understanding.

For my sons, Patrick and Riley — I pray that all of the bumps and bruises born of watching your Momma make her way in this world, fade into a beautiful birthmark on your hearts. You are so loved.

For my daughter, Maggie (my wise-beyond-her-believable-years, Margaret Elizabeth) — Your resilience is miraculous and your spirit is unstoppable. Together, we have stumbled through some pretty rough stuff, but you have shown me that there is magic in making the stumble part of the dance. I am lucky and humbled to be your mother.

For my God, my awesome God — You waited for me to find You. You reached into the mess that I had made of my life, and saved me from myself. Thank you for holding a space for me by Your side. May I use this life to spread light and love.

For all of the women walking through this wondrous world — May you forever know that you are already enough, and that the boxes that have been built for your dreams and desires are too small. Be big. Be bold. Be brave. Grab with gusto the life of passion and purpose that your heart is longing for. You deserve nothing less, I promise.

And finally, a quiet and special nod to JD for backing my dreams even while thinking that I may be bat-shit crazy — I love you and I hope that you are holding onto my tiger tail until the end of time.

JulieO

Contents

How to Use This Book	7
Overvierw	11
Earliest Dreams	14
The Power of Our Thoughts and Words	18
Shattering the Glass	22
You are Seaworthy	26
Expanding, Opening and Allowing	32
The Wisdom of the Heart	36
Releasing and Rebuilding	40
The Energy of Anger	44
Crafting a Solid Foundation	48
Uniquely You	52
Finding Passion in Peace	56
Instinctual Wisdom	66
You are Your Perfect Partner	70
Letting Go	74
Surrender and Relief	78
Imagining Abundance	82
Love is the Answer	86
Free to Begin Again	90
About the Author	95

Start anew . . .

"The messages and images of this beautiful book spoke directly to my heart. I shared it with my teenaged daughter, and she couldn't put it down—mesmerized by the unique clarity of the words and pictures. She said it felt healing to read it. I agree. This book is like balm for our hidden wounds. You'll want one to keep and return to again and again…and one to share with anyone you know who has ever been hurt."

—Jill Farmer, author of
There's Not Enough Time
…and other lies we tell ourselves.
JillFarmerCoaching.com

Expect surprises . . .

HOW TO USE THIS BOOK

The text and illustrations found in *You Are Never Broken Beyond Repair: Reclaiming Your Life and Your Light* came to me as a poetic story, and I transcribed the words and created the images as they appeared in my mind's eye. Later, when I began thinking more seriously about pursuing publication, I became concerned that without the addition of some tools to more actively engage the reader, its message may be less effective and impactful.

As I broke down the text and sifted through each page, I added a few questions in an effort to guide the reader toward a tangible and practical application of the text. I then summarized the message of each page, offering concise, clear and powerful words of wisdom.

The book provides room for note taking, but don't be limited by the allocated lines. Grab a journal or notebook and allow your mind and memory to unfold. The chapters themselves are quite small, but the content included is rather large. I would suggest reading the "story" first, while taking a minute or so to see how the artwork speaks to you, relates to your life, and enhances the accompanying text. When you are ready to begin the more active work that the book offers, set aside a block of time, find a quiet spot, and begin the restorative work of reclaiming your life.

Be brave, be bold . . .

OVERVIEW

Are you living the life of your dreams? Are you satisfied and fulfilled at work and at home? Do you wake up most mornings feeling joyous and excited about the day ahead? If the answer to these questions is yes, then you are faring far better than most. So many women today are on autopilot, spinning inside the hamster wheel of busy and never enough. They are exhausted and emotionally emptied. Some struggle with addictions, and others are victims of violence and abuse. Women face illness, death, poverty, divorce and countless other disappointments. Sometimes, sadly, they become defined and derailed by these events. They give up on their deepest desires and abandon the dreams of their heart. The hurts and hardships become a hiding place, an excuse for a half-led life. Allowing bitterness and blame to engulf them, they sleepwalk through a life that they had never planned on living.

In September 2005, deeply entrenched in my battle to overcome depression and anorexia, I received a gift. Without warning or fanfare, a story fell from above, directly into my head. Immediately, and inexplicably, I was compelled to write. Without thought, I watched as my pen poured ink, effortlessly across the paper. Using scrapbook paper that I had on hand, I crafted the illustrations as I had seen them in my mind's eye. Less than four hours later, lay the story that became this book. I was surprised, humbled, blessed and grateful. At the same time, I felt completely inadequate, inferior and ill-prepared. The Wisdom of the Divine had descended upon me, and She lovingly showed me a way out of my mess. She also bestowed upon me a sacred responsibility to share Her story. The book waited patiently beside my bed and in my mind. I knew its message was intended to be shared, but I always found reason for delay. I was not yet ready to usher **Never Broken Beyond Repair: Reclaiming Your Life and Your Light** into the world. Making the book into a tangible reality seemed frightening.

Never Broken Beyond Repair: Reclaiming Your Life and Your Light is a story, a tool to help women to overcome self-defeating beliefs and habits. Page by page, the reader will be led down a path of self-reflection, and then prompted to actively challenge well-worn, maladaptive thought patterns. The book is rich in imagery and metaphors and is intended to be applied to the reader's personal journey. It is broken down into four parts: text; illustration; a series of questions to ponder; and then a pearl of wisdom to punctuate the lesson. Every page encourages introspection and provides an opportunity for the reader to practice a form of "self-led" therapy. **Never Broken Beyond Repair: Reclaiming Your Life and Your Light** is a starting point, a springboard into a place of greater emotional awareness.

Awareness is the genesis of change and is crucial for the actualization of your highest and most authentic self. You are NEVER broken beyond repair. It is NEVER too late to go after your dreams and desires. Renounce the past. Reclaim and remember your story. Step into your power, sing the song of your soul, and watch as the magic unfolds...

Begin . . .

Earliest Dreams

14

Swinging through
the vines of life,
the Woman wants what she
believes she cannot have.

Earliest Dreams

**Dreams give our talents and passions purpose.
Do not allow the limiting beliefs and negativity of others to diminish your destiny.**

Q: *What were your earliest dreams? What did you answer with confidence and excitement when asked, "What do you want to do when you grow up?"*

Who was the first person — that first voice of negativity — who told you that your dreams were unattainable, impractical, or "too big?" Did you abandon your dreams for something "safer" and "more realistic?"

_____
_____
_____
_____
_____
_____
_____
_____
_____
_____
_____
_____
_____
_____
_____
_____
_____
_____
_____

The Power of Our Thoughts and Words

18

Swimming, then sinking in a
bottle of despair,
the Woman struggles
and gasps for a breath of life,
only to choke on blackened emptiness.

The Power of Our Thoughts and Words

Words are powerful.
They can be used as weapons against ourselves
— or they can be purveyors of peace.
Thoughts are also powerful.
If you think that you can,
you are correct.
If you think that you cannot,
you are also correct.
Pay attention to, and carefully guard the
content and quality of your thoughts.

Q: *What words and limiting beliefs fill your "bottle of despair?" What negative messages do you ingest willingly and regularly? Do you listen to, and react to your limiting internal dialog?*

Fear-based lies that we feed ourselves:
- I am not smart enough.
- I am not pretty enough.
- I am not talented or special.
- I am not lucky; things like that only happen to lucky people.
- I don't have time. I have too many other responsibilities.
- I am overweight.
- I am too old.
- I am too young and inexperienced.

Who and what are the burdens, the weights in your life? How many of these burdens are self-imposed? How many have you actually created for yourself?

_____
_____
_____
_____
_____
_____
_____
_____

Shattering the Glass

Fragmented pieces, shattered dreams, scattering
haphazardly. Dreams and destiny, relentlessly
injured by disruption and destruction.

The blood of life begins spilling slowly from the skin's tiny
traumas. She tries to escape, to set herself free, shocked to
discover that her glass house was never truly her home.

Tears of terror and shame fall from her eyes,
washing away the dangerous pieces —
the shards of a shelter that never was.

"You were not to rock the boat!",
a voice screams in horrified remorse.
"Look at what your desires have done —
irreparable damage born of wasted wanting."

**Challenge unfounded fears
in order to create change in your life.**

Q: *What are your external forms of security and validation — your glass house?*

    I have a good job.
    I earn a good income.
    I live in the right part of town — my house is enviable and impressive.
    I drive an expensive and luxurious car.

Is your self-worth deeply rooted and based upon integral character traits, or tenuously floating among external acquisitions and accomplishments?

In order to live the life of your dreams, you must first be comfortable giving voice to those dreams. Are you comfortable sharing your dreams and desires with others, or do you play yourself "small?" Do you sing the song of your heart and speak your truth — or are you afraid to rock the so-called boat?

_____
_____
_____
_____
_____
_____
_____
_____
_____
_____

You are Seaworthy

"Don't you see, you are the boat?"
The Voice of Truth whispers gently in
her ear. "You have been built and then
lovingly rebuilt, piece by piece.

"Every part of you is of great purpose and value.

"You were not created to live inside of
a bottle of false protection — wrongly separated
from your desires — from your destiny.

"You have been placed, and now place yourself,
up on a very high shelf; your life and
the comfort and love of others, just out of reach."

You are Seaworthy

"You, dear woman, are seaworthy.
Set sail and behold
the beauty of your journey."

The Woman-Vessel is frightened by the words
spoken by Wisdom and Truth.
"Where and how do I begin, and
when will my voyage end?" she wonders.
"I don't have a plan, a map, a charted course."

The Woman-Vessel, paralyzed
by her thoughts and fears, half-heartedly
convinces herself that she does indeed
enjoy the sameness and safety of the bottle.

She settles somewhat tentatively
high up on her familiar and stifling shelf —
her dreams and desires sealed away,
corked off from the hope of her heart.

**Fear is harmless until you give it power.
Then, and only then, does it become
an insidious force of stagnation
and a destroyer of dreams.
A "safe" life will never satisfy your spirit.**

Q: *When you are quiet, what does your heart whisper in your ear? Do you listen, or do you allow fear to silence the yearnings and longings of your heart? In what areas of your life do you "play it safe?"*

Expanding, Opening and Allowing

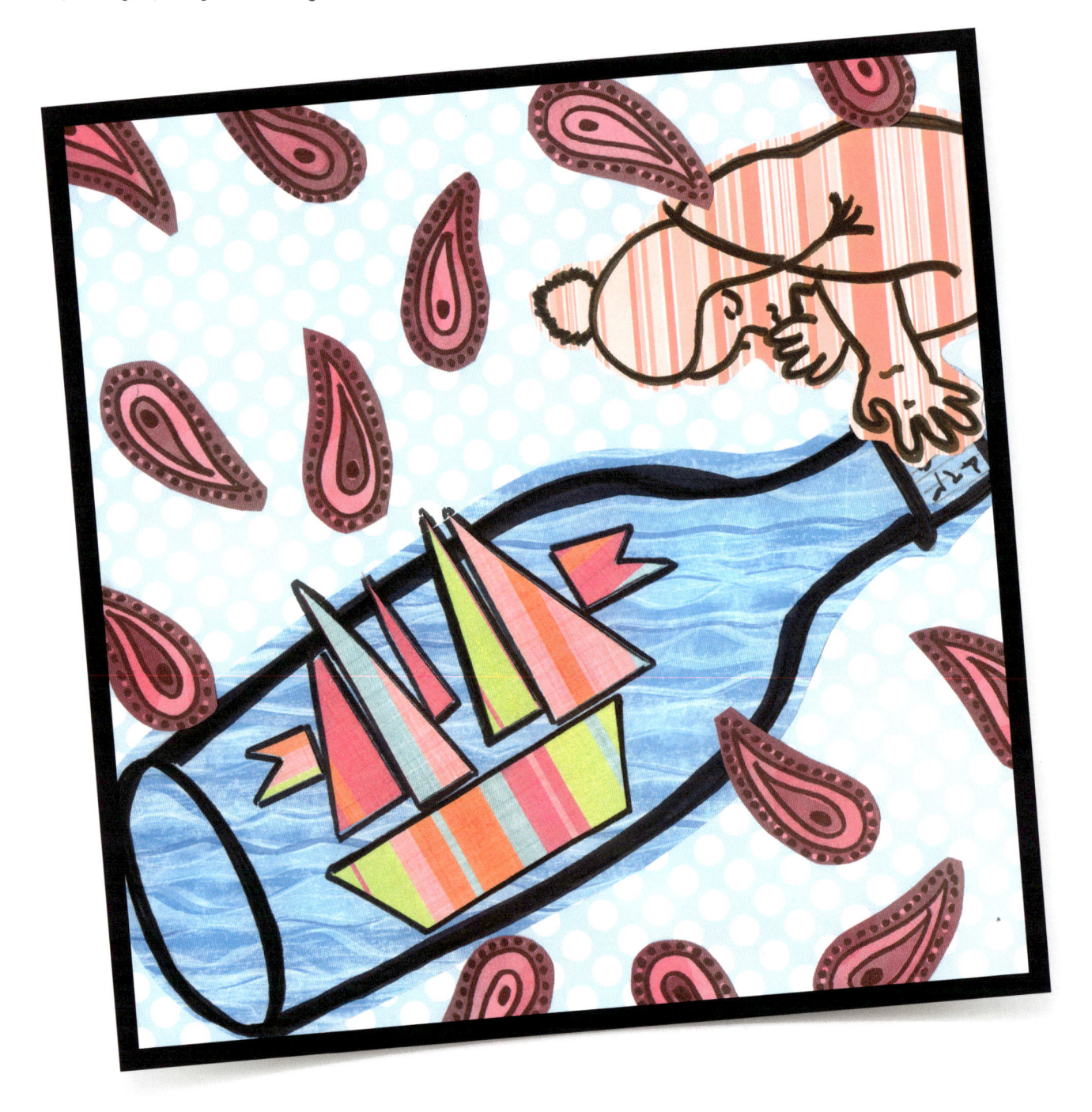

One day, the Woman-Vessel feels a gentle tugging,
followed by an unexpected "whoosh" of fresh, cool air.
Her sails stir as she watches her soft and
tiny hands attempt to touch and feel
the fluttering of the colorful flags.

Triangles of silk, waving to the world — as the
plump fingers of life — born of the Vessel, ache and
struggle longingly. Hands of hope, so desperate to
find a safe passageway and a loving guide.
Sadly, the mouth of the bottle will not open or expand.
Its narrowness obscuring the natural flow of life and love.

The Woman-Vessel is certain that the hands of life
will hurt her, devastate her. Impatient, angry,
smashing hands of past hatred — flashes of painful
violation — relentlessly pulsing through the sea inside.

Expanding, Opening and Allowing

**Embrace the energy of expansiveness.
Do not be afraid to soften and stretch
yourself. Opening your mind and heart
creates room for growth.
Endless possibilities begin
in the fresh and new.**

Q: *Do you ever hear a "whoosh" or feel a tug? This sensation is your higher self, your light, your heart and dreams reminding you — "Don't abandon me. I am waiting …"*

You will never hear the "sound of self" if you busy yourself endlessly, or anesthetize your soul with technology, food, sex, shopping or alcohol.

In what ways have you narrowed your passageway? Are you holding on to the pain of the past? Do you burden yourself by holding on to anger and resentments? Silencing the screenplay of negativity is a daily choice that requires your attention and tenacity.

_____
_____
_____
_____
_____

Choose a mantra; a concise sentence that rings true for you.

Examples:
    My life is filled with joy and purpose.
    I find new opportunities and excitement each day.
    A loving light shines through me and flows into all of my relationships.

_____

With lipstick, or a dry erase marker, write your mantra across the top of your mirror. Read it aloud daily. Let it infuse and energize your body and spirit.

The Wisdom of the Heart

Wisdom and Truth whisper once again,
"She is waiting ever so patiently.

"Open your heart, the mouth of your vessel,
and allow for the breath of love and life.

"Watch the innocence escaping and tumbling
from her — soft crimson petals —
plump pillows of perfect pink,
healing the pain of the past."

You are born knowing, wise, and wonderful. You hold all of the answers inside of your very own heart.

Q: *How do you tap into your inner wisdom? Do you know what it means to "listen to your heart?" Would you recognize the Voice of Truth if she spoke to you?*

Everyday practices that naturally facilitate a heart connection:
- singing
- dancing
- laughing
- storytelling
- meditation
- spending time in nature
- writing, journaling
- sketching, painting, the arts

Releasing and Rebuilding

The Woman-Vessel lets go at long last.
The dam gives way, and a life-altering undercurrent unleashes powerful waves of wisdom and want.
The now unstoppable momentum of desire crashes from stem to stern.

Rivers of sorrow and rivulets of hope fall from the once darkened portholes, releasing and rebuilding simultaneously.

Releasing and Rebuilding

Tears wash away pain, and water
the garden of spirit and soul.
Tears are reminders of the beauty
and fragility of humanity.

Q: *Who or what is darkening your "portholes," obstructing the view of your victorious vision?*

What beliefs do you hold about crying? Do you cry at all? Do you let others see you cry? Do you consider crying to be a "waste of time" or a "sign of weakness?" What messages did you receive as a child regarding tears and crying?

_____
_____
_____
_____
_____
_____
_____
_____
_____
_____

Crying is an invaluable part of releasing pain. Crying cleanses and comforts our souls, and is a natural part of the human experience. Without this crucial emotional cleansing, we are subject to misplaced anger and emotional exhaustion. Bottling our emotions is damaging. Eventually, inevitably, we splinter and crack. Not feeling comfortable, capable or confident expressing our truth — sharing our feelings, dreams and desires — robs us of our individuality and personal integrity.

The Energy of Anger

The Woman-Vessel becomes childlike in her
thoughts and fears. She sees herself as unchristened
and unable to set sail. The river rises rapidly,
and she feels it imperative to quiet and quell
the unfamiliar storms of life and love.

Despite her great efforts to slow the swell,
the river continues its rising and raging.
Her tears slow, but refuse to cease.
Her efforts to stop the flow are wasted
as she sheds thick and sticky tears.

The Vessel shudders and struggles in a frustration
and fear so great — unleashing a fierce anger — energy that
catapults the craft onto dry and barren land.

Anger is often a mask for sadness.
When you find healthy ways to express
both, the joy and satisfaction in your life
will increase exponentially.

Q: *What are your beliefs about anger? Do you view anger as something to be avoided or suppressed? Are you ever surprised by your anger? Is your anger the silent and simmering kind, or the raging, and unexpectedly explosive kind? Is your anger helping you, or hurting you and your relationships?*

_____
_____
_____
_____
_____
_____
_____
_____
_____
_____
_____
_____
_____
_____

When properly directed and expressed, anger can be healthy and even motivating. Anger calls us to action and is often the impetus for change. It is possible to communicate angry feelings in a loving way. Healthy communication of anger is crucial to the success and satisfaction of your relationships. Pay attention to your choice of words, tone and volume. Avoid over-generalizations, eye-rolling, sarcasm and name-calling.

Crafting a Solid Foundation

"Safe at last," thinks the Woman-Vessel,
relieved to be free from the terrifying
waters of an uncharted course.

The repressed fears and bottled disappointments
continue to push from within the galley of
the Woman-Vessel as darkened drops of half-life spill
onto the dry patch of earth, the foundation of false
security on which the Woman-Vessel now docks.

The waters of regret fall onto the cracked and barren soil,
creating a stagnant puddle of muck and pain.
The once shining ship — dulled and deadened by the
dirt of unfulfilled desires — abandons herself,
leaving her broken remains alone and unattended.

The body is the temple for your spirit and soul. Treat it lovingly, and feed it with enriching nourishment. Your environment is a reflection of your internal state, allow only what is functional and beautiful to remain.

Q: *What are some of the ways in which you abandon yourself daily? Are you eating a healthy diet? Do you get enough exercise and sleep? Do you overextend yourself to others? Do you have a hard time saying "no?" Has your body, your home, or both become "dulled and deadened?" What are your greatest disappointments? Do you blame or shame yourself when recalling these disappointments, or are you able to glean a lesson from them, and use them as tools for learning?*

_____
_____
_____
_____
_____

There are many foundations of false security:
- Physical beauty
- A taut and toned physique
- A relationship/marriage
- A secure job
- A well-crafted image of financial status and success

What qualities and character traits would you choose to be the building blocks of your foundation?

_____
_____
_____

Uniquely You

52

Without her sails, her boards and planks, the Vessel moves invisibly through night and day — through life and death. She believes that she is safe at last, free from the burdens of her colorful and weighty mast. Sadly, and much sooner than the Woman-Vessel anticipates, she feels lost and lonely. "Who am I," she asks herself, "without my silk sails above, without the wet hands of life supporting me from below?"

Anchor-less and alone, she wanders back to the forgotten Vessel. She patiently — and ever so carefully — repairs the splits and splinters of neglect, overuse and abuse.

With focused determination,
she gently pulls herself to the water's edge.

Abandoning your unique "colors" creates a deep sense of loneliness and isolation.

Q: *Can you recall a time in your life when you chose to dull the vibrancy of your sails? Do you camouflage parts of yourself in an attempt to "fit in?" What parts of yourself do you disown, or try to hide from others?*

Finding Passion in Peace

A pile of rocks and broken concrete
lie just off to her right; debris dumped thoughtlessly
where it did not belong. Ignorance and careless humanity,
marring the beauty of Mother Nature.

The Woman-Vessel approaches a glorious and
brilliant color with interest and respect.
She lowers herself slowly, and as she does,
a passionflower turns its head.

Their eyes meet and lock as they recognize
each other as long-ago forgotten friends.
Why they had parted ways was no longer important.

Compassionately, the Woman-Vessel begins to remove the
heavy rubble from around the stem and stamen.

"**Stop!**" cries the stoic stalk of life, urgently.
"Without these burdens,
I will lose the strength born of struggle.

"Without these obstacles, I am certain
to lose my will to live, my drive to survive.
I know nothing of the soil of peace; the ground
beneath me has been forever fraught with fear."

"The beauty of my buds —
the intensity and depth of my color —
is birthed from a long and labored past."

To be without this struggle, the passionflower fears
stagnation, disappointment and disillusionment.
The leaves of life begin folding, and crumbling —
her stem halved — collapsing headfirst into the earth.

You are never broken beyond repair.
Your soul is impervious to pain, your
spirit is endlessly buoyant and resilient.

Q: *What debris, both internal and external, is cluttering your mind and your life? Do you believe that you work best "under pressure?" Do you allow, or invite unnecessary chaos into your life? Are you making excuses, or seeking validation by telling yourself and others the "story" of your busy day? How does living a chaotic life serve you? Is life happening to you, or are you making your life happen?*

___

A busy and chaotic life is often unbalanced and unnerving. Chronic chaos makes emotional connection to yourself and others almost impossible.

Pressure creates stress and weakens integrity, functionality and durability.

Leaning into Love

Moments later, a Great Light
illuminates the blue sky,
blanketing the Vessel of Life and
the seeds of desire.

A surge of peaceful love — a comforting calm —
warms them from within. The storm has passed,
and the flower of the future watches
excitedly as the Woman-Vessel sets sail.

Quiet reflection cultivates health,
healing and well-being, allowing you
to regroup and renourish.
Life and love flourish in peace and light.

Q: *How do you experience "great light" and love in your life? Do you have a rich spiritual life and faith in the Divine? Do you have an understanding of the ways in which religion and spirituality are different from one and other? Do you actively create pockets of peace in your day?*

Instinctual Wisdom

Just above on the horizon,
the sun begins its daily descent;
a ball of fiery blazing glory,
reliably returning to the heart of the sea.

As the fingers of light delicately touch the water,
a lone wolf howls in the distance. Her strong and
mighty cries of instinct, circle the earth.

Deep and determined eyes speak of everlasting vigilance.
"I am hunting," the She-Wolf howls. "I am fighting to
ensure our survival." Sinewy ropes of muscle, taught and
readied, prepared to prowl and pounce at any moment —
her instincts effortless — her protection natural.

**As you return to your center,
clarity reawakens your instincts
and personal power.**

Q: *Deep within you, lies your natural instinct. Do you trust your intuition? Do you listen to your "gut?" Can you remember a time in your life when you just "knew" something although you could not explain how? Was there ever a time when you ignored your sixth sense? When and why did you stop trusting yourself?*

You are Your Perfect Partner

The night continues to wake, and a
creature of snow white magnificence appears,
its rider seated in a proud and brave wisdom.

"As she is your instinct," a gentle voice speaks
of the wolf, "I am your heart, the keeper of light.
We are fearless. We are eternal, our constant
abundance ensuring your life." A wise wolf and
a woman warrior — hand in hand — making a
life of fear and loneliness forever an impossibility.

As you open your heart and heal from the pain of your past, you return to your natural and original state of self-love and acceptance; this is your birthright. Self-love obliterates loneliness. Be your own best friend.

Q: *Are you comfortable doing things alone? Do you feel lonely when you are by yourself? Do you enjoy your own company, or do you feel that you need another person to complete you or validate your life experiences? Do you refer to your partner as your "better half," or are you searching for your "other half?" Healthy and wholly satisfying relationships will not happen until you are wholly healed and have a loving relationship with yourself. A whole person — living a whole life — attracts others who are healed and whole.*

Letting Go

The She-Wolf, sated by her journey and nourished by her conquests and accomplishments, follows the heart to their home. As they turn the last corner, the eyes of the Wolf light up in delight as she rests her gaze upon her pack, the life of her loins. Wonder and pride swell, and the She-Wolf rejoins the circle of life and love. Secure and protected, unshackled and free, the She-Wolf lies down among her own.

With that, the Male stirs and shivers; her return signaling both an end and a beginning, a change of seasons. He rises and prepares for his departure, his inevitable journey into what could be a long and arduous winter. Tears wet the earth as their eyes meet, and the She-Wolf lays down in love, Home at last.

Letting Go

**One diseased or deadened branch
can poison an entire tree.
Lop off — cut out — the people and habits that
are inhibiting your growth, and diminishing
the bounty and succulence of your fruits.**

Q: *Who or what do you need to let go of in your life?*
What is keeping you from the "life of your loins?"

Surrender and Relief

Suddenly, the sky opens as the
Universe weeps joyously —
a bottle from above, generously pouring
life into many hardened hearts.

In the cold and empty darkness below,
another bottle shatters, spilling emptiness
into nothingness.

Surrender and Relief

The Universe is conspiring on your behalf. Your fears are paper tigers, figments of past pain veiled in imaginary power.

Q: *Self-acceptance and love shatter darkness, and ameliorate the pain of the past. Are there people in your life who leave you feeling empty? What responsibilities/chores leave you feeling drained and depleted? Can you think of a way to infuse more joy into these activities? What nurturing practices can you incorporate into your daily life?*

_____
_____
_____
_____
_____
_____
_____
_____
_____
_____

Examples:
- Light a candle.
- Take a warm and fragrant bath.
- Listen to soothing music.
- Prepare a delicious meal.
- Take a gentle walk.
- Schedule a massage.
- Forgive yourself for past mistakes.

Imagining Abundance

A beautiful, voluptuous,
miraculous woman
dances freely
among the flowers.

Your life is a garden of your own creation. Visualize the life of your dreams, and trust that the Wisdom of the Divine will show you the way. Joy is infectious, so dance. As you do, you remind others to recall and to reclaim the song of their heart.

Q: *What kinds of music or types of activities excite you and make you feel alive? What "flowers" do you want to plant in your life? Take the time to think very specifically about this question. Close your eyes, and begin to imagine the garden of your life. Where is it located? What does it look, sound and smell like? What grows with ease and abundance in your garden?*

_____
_____
_____
_____
_____
_____
_____
_____
_____
_____
_____
_____
_____
_____
_____
_____
_____
_____
_____

Love is the Answer

A tiny, innocent hand rests, nestled safely
in the hands of Gentle Wisdom.

Side-by-side, mother and child, present and
future, dream and desire, walk along
the shore; their eyes are drawn to a
beautiful boat on the horizon.

An endless sphere of incandescent light
glows, and warms the peaceful pack…

Love heals all hurts.
Love can change your life.
Love has the power to change the world.
Love is a daily choice, and love begins with you.

Q: *Where do you find comfort in your life? Are you able to soothe yourself? Take a moment to close your eyes and imagine yourself as a child — feeling alone or afraid. What comforting words or phrases did you need to hear in order to feel safe and supported? Now, take a moment to soothe yourself with those words. Wrap your arms around her and hold her — send her your unconditional love.*

Free to Begin Again

...and a heart on a horse spreads its wings and soars straight into a beautiful beginning.

Free to Begin Again

**Living in light and love, unshackled and unburdened
from the old, you are free to begin again.
Plant a new garden.
Cultivate your dreams, and dust off your desires.
See the magnificent possibilities glimmering
on the horizon, and reclaim your Spirit.
Make a list. Chart a course.
Shatter the bottle, and remember the dream
that your heart never forgot.**

Q: *How and where do you want to create new beginnings in your life? What steps can you take to initiate these beginnings? What supports do you need in place, to be successful in the implementation of these changes?*

ABOUT THE AUTHOR

Julie O'Connor is an artist, entrepreneur, motivational speaker and survivor. After recovering from a chronic and life-threatening eating disorder, she began sharing her story with other girls, teens and women. She has spoken in residential treatment facilities, high schools and at continuing education conferences for psychiatrists, psychologists, and other mental health professionals.

Julie has also worked as a recovery coach for patients transitioning from inpatient care in to a less structured level of support. Julie was victimized by rape and abuse, but she is not a victim. Her story has been a beacon of hope for females who feel marred and scarred by trauma, and for teenage girls struggling with addiction, body image and self-esteem issues.

Among Julie's personal and professional goals is a deep desire to serve and to play a part in the healing and unification of women as a gender. "United, we are powerful beyond measure, and divided, we are dangerous," is Julie's call for women to gather as sisters, share their stories, and assist one another on the journey toward emotional and spiritual advancement and healing.

Unpack and let the journey begin . . .

I am so grateful that I was able to share a part of my heart with you, and I invite you to share a part of your heart with me as well.

JulieO

Julie@JulieOJourneys.com

CPSIA information can be obtained at www.ICGtesting.com
Printed in the USA
LVIW01n0923070416
482404LV00003B/3